THE
UPSIDE-DOWN
TREE

THE
UPSIDE-DOWN
TREE

Poems

by

Jean Janzen

HENDERSON
BOOKS

Winnipeg, Manitoba
Canada

Published by Henderson Books,
a division of Windflower Communications, Winnipeg, Manitoba.

Canadian Cataloguing in Publication Data

Janzen, Jean
  The upside-down tree: poems
  ISBN 0-929130-05-7 (bound) -- 0-929130-03-0 (pbk.)

I. Title.
PS3560.A5j9U67 1992   811'.54 C92-098085-6

Acknowledgements
Some of the poems in this collection first appeared in the following magazines:
The Antioch Review, Arete, Common Wages, Festival Quarterly, The Gettysburg Review, Journal of Mennonite Studies, Mennonite Life, The New Quarterly, The Pacific Review, Poet Lore, Prairie Schooner, Quarry West, and *The Rolling Coulter.*
Three poems were included in the anthology, *Piecework: 19 Fresno Poets.*

Special thanks to Louis Janzen, and to Peter Everwine, Dixie Lane, Roberta Spear and Robert Vasquez for their help and support.

Artwork by Spencer Newel, Fresno, CA.

International Standard Book Number: Paperback 0-929130-03-0
International Standard Book Number: Cloth   0-929130-05-7

FOREWORD NOTES

"I have looked forward to seeing Jean Janzen's new collection of poetry for some time, and I am not disappointed. The poems in *The Upside-Down Tree* are richly textured pieces, full of the play of light and darkness, like trees, in full, leafy celebration, all shade and brilliance, squirrels, cardinals, hidden fruits, and, just to make sure we remember where and who we are, a dirty T-shirt or some equally important human artifact left hanging from a branch. With her consummate skill, she creates not only pictures with her words, but re-creates Rembrandt and Vermeer, draws us unto words, into the sensual reality of everyday life around and between the words. She bears a flickering candle for those who dwell in darkness, and a flickering darkness for those who blunder about in the light. She takes not only her experience and that of her generation, but reaches back into Mennonite history to make these people real, complex and fully human. For those of us used to reading dry or self-righteous histories, it is a wonderful, welcome surprise."

David Waltner-Toews

"These poems are tributes to people who were members of the poet's immediate family and of a larger group — the Mennonites, whose migrations spanned three continents as they fled from persecution and poverty. The strength, vision and deep faith of these people are at the core of every poem. It seems extraordinary that, in the entire collection, there is never a false note, an un-earned embellishment. If there is an unnerving quality in the work, it is the sense of serenity which is unalterable and luminous — something that comes only when one has learned how to survive the pain of life as well as how to honor its gifts."

Roberta Spear

for my mother and in memory of my father

Contents

Part One

Part Two

Part Three

Part Four

Part One

POTATO PLANTING

All you need is one good eye,
he said in the still chilly spring,
his spade making soft, black holes.

The cut pieces soon stir
with that nourishing fire
like those losses we think

we bury for good, that begin
to smolder in their dark sleep
and extend their thin, white roots.

What is visible flourishes.
Under the glare of the sun
potato plants push out

their rough tongues and make
their easy promises. Not until
the fall digging do we see them,

whole families of pale,
forgotten children coming home
at dusk, blackened

by the coal mines, waiting
to be washed and held,
begging for their stories to be told.

UNDER THE BRILLIANT SNOWS
OF CHILDHOOD

Autumn's dark angles
were covered with
the muffling beauty.
All that feathery play!
But the glare
brought our eyes to tears
like teacher's hard looks.
Mother's window sheers
kept nothing out,
flaws in the carpet
and on my face
so sharply illuminated.
That unforgiving light
on the page of Chopin,
a winter landscape wooded
with accidentals.
The slippery left hand.
Now winter lies in variations
of brown and gray, earth
bare and open.
My rooms are muted by the low
sun's dark absorption.
The body knows a softening,
a gathering toward
dim light.
Lamp in the corner,
sound of rain wetting me down
with its knowledge.

After we buried my father,
I let the water run hard
into the tub to drown out
my sobbing. But I
can still hear it,
and, now and then,
on first warm days,
melting snow
in an icy trickle
under the drifts.

BAPTISM

Mother tells me
of her fear that
the swift river
would tear her
from the chain of wet
human hands,
this river that recirculates
the water of the world,
even the sorrow
from the other side.
She tells me how she
braced herself
against the current
and affirmed
her single heart,
her voice blending
into the water's wild
chorus.
     We stand
on the bank looking down,
our feet in the ancient Indian
trail rutted by the loaded
dragboards, the river
their guide,
witness of autumn
pushing at their backs,
the benevolent summer god
yielding to the hoary-headed
one.

The water
flows south. Mother,
you could have let go
and let it carry you,
the dark ribbon cutting
ever deeper into
the earth. But you
took your stand
and then came up with
the others. All the joined
hands, the sturdy stake
driven into the bank.

DOUBLE RAIL

Winter 1933 and one more mouth
to feed. Seven at home and his schoolroom
full during freeze and thaw. I wonder
what he wanted then as he crossed
the darkening yard where after lessons
he skated with the growing boys. I wonder
what he thought when he entered the warm
kitchen where my mother waited, her apron clean,
dark hair smooth, skin smelling of bread.
What to give a woman when she asks?

Refuge? A thousand years of peace?
Only after the Rapture, he tells my brothers
at the supper table. Premillenialism,
he called it. (And the young child
listens and fears, for who can abide
the day of His coming?)
His broad, immaculate hands butter
the bread, the talk is steady. What difference,
the train stopping at Karkhoff with the Reds
streaming out, or the S.S. blowing bridges
in the spring? Sons. Brothers. Nothing
to stop the flow. A train for escape?
Zug, we called it in German,
as it dragged through the prairie, sighing
into the station with its load.

*

The congregation stares up at him
in the pulpit. Behind him the words
carved on the wall: *Heaven and earth
shall pass away*, as the corn swells
and the lake thickens with fish. In the pews
all of us listening for the Word that speaks
to our feasts and droughts, to the sludgy
bottom of the lake and the silence after harvest.

This life is a journey to another world,
a different glory, he sang out as he stood
shaving at the mirror. He rode the trains
with a carefree spirit, at country crossings
inched the car forward toward the thundering freight
as we gasped and begged. But also, he knew
the shadowy places, the times when life was stopped
and crowded, when he confided, *sometimes I
hardly know who I am*. That great distance
and my mother kissing him, so that at the end
he wasn't sure to which home he wanted to go.

QUESTIONING THE COLD

Every summer in Saskatchewan
northern lights play over the graves
of my ancestors, magnetic forces
a hundred miles up energized
in the great frozen heights.
Children stand in their nightclothes
and wonder, then dream of angels,
ghosts of old glaciers.

In this cold country
do Grandfather's bones ever really thaw?
Does his white hair still gleam
in the blackness?

I never knew his arms.
And now I stand between him
and this high magic, alone
in my warm skin.
The colored light-bands
flick their icy tongues over me.
Is this the language of glacier
and iceberg, or of stars and heaven?
Can holy be warm? Was Job right
about the flesh?

PEACHES IN MINNESOTA

Mrs. Nachtigal, Mrs. Peters, and Mrs. Tieszen
each in their separate steamy kitchens
ripped the slats off the perfect rows
of peaches and said as they bent over, plump
and panting, not to eat a single one fresh.
These rows of peach buttocks, the skins
turning rosy after the long train ride
from California in the refrigerated miracle car,
were now in the hands of Mrs. Nachtigal,
Mrs. Peters, and Mrs. Tieszen who said no,
not one. First the scalding dip
to slip off the furry skins, then the quick
slice to take out the pit, the careful slide
and pour into the Mason jars, the steam bath
until the lids snapped in with their safe
seals, and then the shining rows on the drainboard,
breasts of peaches under glass to be brought up
from the dank cellar when it was time,
the syrupy flesh delicious in the mouth
as snow ticked against the windows, cherished
like the low sun of January. Altogether different
from California where we eat them ripely sweet
from the tree all summer long, whenever we
have the urge, and as many as we want, even as
the fallen ones rot in the hot furrow, and
the air conditioner hums and hums in monotone.

WHITE

She could lose them all
in the blizzards as they slip
off the icy ropes. This one,
a few weeks old, lies in a coffin,
his cheek on the iron-cold satin
of her wedding dress.

Winter stands by
wearing her long, white ermine
buttoned up tight
over the breathing hills
and heartbeat, her glazed face
turned away.

In a dream the house
was suddenly banked
with masses of white flowers,
and the baby white and lost
among them until his mouth
pinked with a cry.

She wants winter
to give herself up,
to open her gown
and give him back
from the folds of her body,
which, under its locks of ice,
holds what we need,
even in its darkest place.

THE CLARITY OF DIRT

A woman sits by late lamplight
planting violets on bonnets
with her needle. Today she pressed
sheets and pillowcases, white

with roses on the borders. Soon
the harvesters will come in.
Too exhausted to wash,
they will lie down on those

linens, the dirt making prints
of their bodies. And they
will dream with a certain clarity.
Like the blind man with mud

on his eyes, they will see trees
walking like men. They will
rise up to meet them, lifting
their loads easily, as in

a dance. And she will dream
that the meadow has come into
her house, that she is floating
on it, her children running

freely with muddy feet
over her sheeted body. All of them
in this night-darkened house
knowing in their sleep

why they are here, what they
were meant to be.

FOX

You want it to happen
in the wild, not in your
trimmed yard—the leap
and kill. Feathers
of a coddled duck, and then
another and another, pale
down of the young ones,
iridescence of the mallard's
neck swirling around you.
And then from the arbor
the fire of his gaze—a fox
in his coat of gray and orange.
Summer nights you hear
his harsh barking, and in
your bed of love and loss
you dream that his elegant tail
circles your neck. Unlike
the ladies of your childhood,
the winter ladies in their buttoned
coats, you are naked and he
is alive, his breath against
your breasts, his small sharp teeth,
as in the fowl-pen the bones
of the goose lie pale and serene,
wing-tips stretched against the earth.

OSPREY

We drive through the coastal redwood
forest in a low glide, through a tunnel
of shade, tires hushed by the thick robes

and shaggy arms overhead. A peaceful tribe,
undisturbed for a thousand seasons.
Then, suddenly, among the green towers,

a triumvirate of dead trees pierces
a patch of sky, and at the pinnacle of one,
an osprey stands by her nest,

a jumbled palace of twigs. She releases
a series of shrieks that rip the silence.
Announcements. Revelations. Something

about the nakedness of her nest, how it
nearly kindles at noon, how it darkens
with rain. She flaps her bent, black wings.

Her vision is sharpening:
beyond the trees, rocks are crumbling
and falling, and above them

is the blue passage where the upsurge
almost carries her away, and there, a gleam
that shifts and disappears. Her hooks

move in and out, her feathers shine.
The forest is dark with secrets, the stream
pouring from its scented shade is narrow,

the fish are quick and slippery,
and they flash like silver.

BEFORE SLEEP

All day the ocean asked
the same questions.
There at the edge of the cliff
where the car doors flew open,
our children spilled out to play,
to scramble wet rocks in high wind,
and at times we lost sight of them.
Today among the roar the gray whales
breached and blew northward,
their calves following close.
A child of the plains, I couldn't imagine
these glittering fields
or that rise of slippery mass
above them. Again and again
we asked each other, "Did you see,"
and followed their spouts until
they disappeared into the dusk.
The limestone hollows echoed
as the water pulled away
from the cliffs, and we returned
to our room where last night
we saw the moon hang her sickle-light
over the high breakers
as we stood arm in arm.

Were they ready for this undertow,
those endless miles of shine,
this wind that drenches
the leaning cypresses? Those dark bodies
tumble northward as our own fall
into drowsiness, and we ride once again
our mother's heartbeat, serene
in her steerage. Her lungs fill
and empty over me, and tonight
I think I hear her singing.

FLOAT

When I jumped,
my body opened and fell
into the emptiness, fast
and soundless, until
the rip and flap of the parachute,
the float, the fields
rising up to meet me.

But this is a lie.
It was my son who told me,
I'm going fishing, then jumped
into those clear columns of air.

Who can bear to tell the truth,
or hear it? All night long
the torrent in your ears,
rush of wind before you find shelter.
But in the half-light of dawn
you almost believe that the air
holds you, dreaming again
of the stranger who rescues you
from the crowd, then lifts
you in a joyful float
above the city—hair flying,
cheek against his coat—
until the sun burns
through the last veil.
Then the body falls full-weight
and the voices grow dim.
Songs about letting go,
about fishing in the sky.

for Scott

Part Two

RECLAIMING THE LAND

1

Not even Kansas is as flat as this place,
our eyes interrupted only by the distant
dikes where a sailboat is a speck
floating above the land. Land and sea,
elemental, separated as in God's third day.
Order out of chaos. And great emptiness.

Twelfth Century, Hadewijch the Mystic gathers
the young sisters around her, pleads
with them to cherish their emptiness,
to be tender toward their human longings.
They stand in a huddle in the marshy field.
The tree is upside-down, she says, eyes
searching, hats and skirts flapping.
Inside, that burning.

2

These are my people near the breaking
rage of the North Sea, and inland
by the quiet avenues of water —

Menno Simons' escape routes
and his arteries of faith. What footings
here for the descendants,

what moorings for the heavy cargo
of ourselves? The light stays long
in the Dutch summer. Green promises

more green even as I sleep. This land,
reclaimed, opens and fills — country manors,
barns, ships that sailed away and returned

heavy-laden, captains that demanded
blood, and these people with my name
refusing, cutting the ropes, letting it go.

3
"Mennoniten? Sie spielen nicht,
sie trinken nicht, sie lachen nicht,"
say our friends from across the Ems.
Separation from the world? The words
shift like global waters, mirror
the fickle sky.

The land lies uneasily
beside the ocean's strength.
Winds strain at the locked gears
of windmills. One sweeps and dries
the damp fields, another
carries floods in its arms.
Which wind? Which true one
for the turning?

4

In his "View of Haarlem"
Ruisdael's sky dominates
the land. Great thunderheads
rise over the far dikes, faces
of beauty and danger over
the fields of grain, the red
slanted roofs, the dark clusters
of elms and chestnuts.
What we want is hidden,
something elemental that stirs
in the color or in the canvas
itself. Something under
those long stretches of white
linen drying in that shaft
of sunlight.

FLOWERS OF AMSTERDAM

For the sake of the Gospel,
the book says. 1549. Pieter, Johann
and Barbara are tied to the stake.
Their bodies flare out in a triple bloom,
still flare out in the mind, the recalcitrant
flesh still acrid. And Catherine drowns
in the canal, her skirts billowing out
over her tied legs like a lily.

Now vast markets of flowers, a harbor
where once a shipload of grain
was exchanged for a single tulip bulb.
City of night when the streets open
their black laps for the painted blooms,
when music rides the blue and swollen veins,
washed and languid houses that double
in the watery streets.

City of choices. Which fire, which perfume,
and at what price? Catherine cries out
over the water. Each one must choose,
she calls into our bright throats,
each one for himself. And how
do you choose when a whirlpool sucks you in,
into the purple corridors of the iris,
the cool swarm of apple orchards?
"Careful of the feast's tomorrow," Van Gogh
writes near the end, after the yellow skies.
"For my own work I am risking my life,
and my mind is half-gone. . . But what do you want?"

What do you want? The one way to live,
the one unequivocal rose in this life
of mirrors, in this city of water where
the day is now nearly gone and the floodgates
already open. The dark elms dip their hair
into the rising tide and the laden boats
drift with the current. But here and there
one moves against it, one figure in a boat,
the twin oars quietly opening the water's
glistening petals, opening a secret passage
in the deep and watery place.

THE HIDDEN

"Cleave the wood, I am there."
             The Apocryphal Gospel of St. Thomas

1
Each day they would decide,
agonizing, which books to burn
to keep from freezing.
Amsterdam, 1944, and Jan, my friend,
was ten. Jews were hiding
in the false ceiling over the family bookstore,
over the layers of pages
that flared and smoked —
the pure abstractions of math,
Darwin's theories, the engravings
of trees — unfolding against his blue fingers.
Then, late, the dark staircase
to share what had been found.
One night an onion, he remembers.
Each person held the translucent layers
almost reverently. One by one,
torn away, until the center
which was nothing but one more layer,
and tenderest of all.

2
This flat countryside with nothing
to hide, the canals like open cuts
where our ancestors risked their night journeys.
The upturned arms of elms where
they were hung. Rembrandt's open face,
the pain going in and in, then emerging
as light. His mother reading the Bible:
what is hidden, what is revealed.
"You cannot see God and live."
His splendor, we say, or is it
the depth of his sorrow? A tree
wrenched open, the chainsaw limb after limb,
the sap running its curves, running out.

THREE WINDMILLS

1

Inside this windmill
all is clack and thump,
a great stomping of small red seeds
for a trickle of oil. The vanes
turn and turn: light and shadow,
light and shadow, straining and creaking
as they try to lift me from this land.

2

The ones on the midwestern plains
clapped their metal through
those nights without borders,
like the plains themselves,
these mountains a rumor, these rivers
invisible. Only dust and wind
as the windmill clanged on, its song
a monotone about insatiable thirst.

3

The vanes turn and turn,
perhaps to start something new.
Rilke writes, patience is everything,
the German *gedult*, like a duck
too fat to fly. Endurance,
the grind of gears. Or was it
gelassenheit with its upward draft?
A floating resignation, arms cutting
deeply into the empty spaces.

ON THE CANAL, BRUGHES

This is what we want,
this tranquil glide
past old brick and glass
in this medieval town
where silt stopped
the flow of gold
and the weeping post
stands deserted,
where the water is glazed
under summer light
and licks the mossy sides.

Here Jan Van Eyck disembarked
with brush and oils
to paint the marriage portrait:
two real people in a real room
with mirror, dog, and candle.
The binding of hands
preserved under luster, and therefore,
loosened into time.

Today this city holds us
in its own slow float,
and like a medievalist
I touch the flesh of your hand
and know it is more than flesh,
that all touch and union radiates
a particular light
in this city of bridges.
That whole, luminous bedroom
still drifting on, the scarlet-
draped bed, shoes in the corner,
the one candle burning.

VERMEER HAD IT RIGHT

Vermeer had it right, I think,
the woman with the jug, a common
kitchen, the light.

Farther south, angels erupted
in lightning skies, saints rose
on clouds, mothers strained their arms
upward, their eyes wild.

Oh, I know, when my child lies dying,
I want the breakthrough. And those days
when everything scrapes and pulls
me down, and yet,

the simple rituals of the house,
the washing up, the kneading, the rising,
the jug of water holding the day's
light. The miracle of air.

Part Three

THIS MOONLESS NIGHT

1

Golden onions high
among the barren trees.
What we put into borscht
is gilded and mounted
on church towers, and at the Czar's
summer house, deep blue
with golden stars. Four Evangelists
around the large center onion
of Jesus — clear profiles against
the clouded sky, the stories
that we peel, layer after layer,
our eyes smarting with the earthy
fragrance, the tang of the mystery.

2

The ancient monastery stands
in a sprinkle of snow. Stone
crosses, steps, thick walls
with openings for the view.
Imagine the monks looking down
on the winding river and the small
villagers. One remembers
his mother's back as she bent
over the oven for the loaves.
He thinks how he was conceived
in hunger. He wonders that we eat
Christ's body with our bodily
appetites, even for our absolution,
here on this windy hill, each of us
hungering for another, those
crushed kernels of self-giving,
that intimacy, which feeds us.

3

Too early for *troikas*
they say and so we walk
on the muffled streets
in the snow that falls
on the Kremlin Wall
on Lenin's tomb
on Ivan's church
on his great bell
that never rang
it falls
on the potato stand
on all the women
waiting in line
on the evergreens
on my hair
it falls
and we walk in the snow
because the *troikas*
aren't running yet
winter is not quite here
and the wolves are not hungry
enough to begin their howling
in the distant woods

4

Drifting off to sleep you imagine
the next day, what has been planned
for you. Nothing to decide.
Key woman in the hall
watching the doors. Doorman
watching the other doorman.

No moon. No responsibilities.
Like a child you are free
to sleep and dream, and like a child
you will dream the bitter-sweet dreams
of growing up. You will dream
that the key woman is opening
all the doors, and when the fire
breaks out, if you choose the right one,
you will escape.

5

These stands of birches are like music
on a page, or music itself, the delicate
branches drooping and swaying among
the straight trunks of paper-white.
At night, thick by the roadsides
and around country houses, they help
erase the darkness.
I think of the women and children,
the grandfathers, who tried to hide
among them, how they were pushed
from cattle cars onto the empty steppes
of Kazakhstan, how some survived
on field mice in their earthen huts.
Listen to that music.
Chekhov's Masha walks among the trees.
We must live, she says. And the new
generation of birches grows whiter,
even in this moonless night.

PLAIN WEDDING

I try to imagine my grandparents
on their wedding day flying
over the Russian village
with cow and moon. But Chagall's donkey
drops them with a thump.
None of that frivolity,
the fathers said. Black dress
for the bride, like penance
over the apple-breasts.
Hair tightly bound.

What could have lifted them
above the somber wedding sermon
and congregation was song,
that sturdy vine which creeps
and thrusts into the barest room.
Warm voices in four parts
lifting the four corners of paradise
with its lavender skies.
"Grosser Gott, Wir Loben Dich"
washing over them, a purity
of canvas, of bride. Not to be
blemished, but with touch
upon touch, to be filled.

LINES AND STRINGS

for my Grandfather, Peter Wiebe, 1856-1904

As you carved a violin
in the Ukrainian night,

Tchaikovsky up north tangled
with the "Pathetique," all those lines

and strings pulling him on.
And something drew you

to the tension of catgut
over wood, those scraps

you shaped and glued
in the lamplight, even

as the wheat, sown too late,
withered under the moon.

Something—no grand finale
after four movements—

but a single melody that etched
its way into the children's

drowsy heads as they spread
blankets on the dirt floor.

Bloodline and starline
are what you gave me,

one line continuous, the other
breaking off between constellations,

leaving empty spaces in the map's
black sky. Cold places

where sometimes you appear,
tall and bony, scraping your bow

on the bridge. And then
we dance, you and I, tethered,

stepping among the stars.

EATING STONES

for my aunts who died in the Ukrainian
famine in the 1930s

Hunger with its open face,
its open mouth. Simple
as a life-line. I love
the old man's story—
the miracle in the Ukraine—
how that loaf of bread slid off
the military wagon into the snow
and saved his whole family.
Survival and escape from
the unspeakable desert.

One loaf.
When the tramp sat on my
childhood backsteps, hunger
seemed to rub its rags
against the edges of adventure.
The small dramas of the Depression,
my mother exclaiming and clapping
her hands as we opened the huge
round of government cheese.
All of us unaware,
the mute murders so far away.

         I want
history to veer in their behalf,
not that wilderness of stones
with its refusals. Susie, Helen
and Marie, orphaned, young,
and beautiful, emaciated
on the pitiful bedding, their mouths
bloody with the effort. I want
for them the transformation
into loaves. And then, those
other necessities we live by:
a hand on their foreheads,
someone calling them by name.

THE COUSINS

Their hands move across the map.
Here, then here, they say.
Six months on a freight train,
dirt huts on frozen steppes,
the Urals where father starved
to death. Here mother fed pigs,
and here she was imprisoned.
The morning light shifts over us,
Willie's hands so much like my father's,
the fine hairs shining, the curve
of the nails. Here, my father said
to me, a child, breathing beside him:
from Karkhoff to Liebau to Liverpool,
and finally to Quebec, his finger
sliding away over the smooth, pale blue.
*
This Dutch dialect is like a house
I haven't seen since childhood, and we
are reconstructing it with syllables
and hand motions. Beams, struts,
a roof of "Yo" and "Nay,"
timber nearly lost. Now Lena points
past the belching coal stacks —
there is the mine where we worked,
there our first home, fallen
over the collapsing shafts. And there
the tree where we ran and played
with Papa. Papa, who once lay
in a morgue after a beating,
and when he heard voices entering,
he raised his hand. I am alive,
the hand said.
*

Abram has come all the way from Siberia
to meet us. He carries photos.
The album is thin, the pages stacked
with bodies. There they lie
under the muffled ringing of axes,
under moans and mounds of snow,
their pupils fixed like stumps of pine.
The river lies locked and silent,
he says. Nothing but a shriek
of bird, a wing's shadow. Yet sometimes
I hear a creaking, the ice
straining in its gravelly bed.
*

Supper under the summer trees,
melons chilled in well water,
a cup of *kvass* from hand to hand.
Someone remembers a child herding
a flock of geese, or was it
a flight of geese following a thread
of river, tracing it out to sea?
In Willie's lap a mandolin murmurs
the melodies of grasslands, of a windy
sky. Nothing between us now
but our warm breathing, our words
already disappearing.

UP AGAIN

Cat's wails, sirens,
the breaking of glass,
no matter which city,
means the shattering of sleep.
I awaken to these in Karaganda
and rise from a lake of dreams,
think riots, thieves, the KGB,
but see nothing, only stark
moonlight on pale shards.

Karaganda means "black hole,"
cousin Kolya has told me, these acres
of emptiness over a gutted earth,
coal stacks spewing black ribbons
day and night. Near here
Aunt Margaret and her children
were pushed off freight cars
onto the plains. Autumn 1942,
a dirt hut quickly dug
before the blizzards, a diet
of vermin, and hymns rising
in the dark, tones they clung to
like a rope. Finally a drift
of sleep like threads
until baby's cry, or her own muffled
cry, and she was up again,
bare feet on this cold earth.

Now the cool tile under my feet,
and silence, before I lie down
again into the tidal sounds
of the years, that chain of *Kyries*
and the answering *Gott ist die Liebe,*
moonlit and swirling in the dark.

NOT ONLY THE PLOW

Here by the Dnieper River
our ancestors first
made a living raising silkworms.

After several hard winters,
mulberry trees began fattening
the caterpillars,

and the weaver's shuttles
flew. I try to imagine
my greatgrandfather's hands

gently grazing
the shimmering lengths,
his fingertips purple

with dye, how he saved
the best swatch for his daughter's
wedding dress, for the fine

slope of her hips.
And when they prayed for rain,
it was not for those coarse

stalks of wheat,
as we did, but for the deep
roots of trees,

for that pale green unfolding
so that those ravenous worms
could fill and fill,

54

then wrap themselves
in threads of sleep,
to be buried in dreams,

to awaken new,
and then to be held
in the soft arms of the air,
amen.

SILVER APPLES

at the Dnieper River Dam

We know that each bite
holds its histories, both
sweet and bitter,

here at the Dam where water
spills silver in the sun.
We know that the mammoth columns

hold skeletons of people
who fell, famished and exhausted
with labor, men and women

whose names I've heard,
their bodies electrifying
Stalin's world. Fruit

of the harnessed river,
of the stolen light.
Now this thundering,

like a great rumble of laughter.
The spray rises and dissipates
like the blooms in the cemetery

nearby where one stone reads
"No more night" under the dates,
1790-1821, the struggled life

suddenly poured out,
the body's tree planted entire.
Root and crown given up

to the Maker, whose moon
has begun to rise and soon
will rain its silver over all.

FLYING WITH THE LIGHT

In America geese fly
already roasted to your table,
Grandfather told his restless children.
Even in Kiev, the swirl
of feathers, the golden-crusted thigh,
the promise of a better place.
Now in 2 a.m. moonlight the small plane
lofts us out of Zaporoshya,
over fields of sunflowers and coal mines,
over the pure peaks of the Alataus.
Just yesterday our boat churned
a white wake over the old village
of Einlage. Its rutted streets
lay far below us, its broken
picket fences, mattresses slashed
and stained, and the pear trees
gesturing wildly as they are dragged away.
Now moonlight covers the past
like starched linen. The whole earth
shines and hums in my veins,
and I am giving myself to the cool,
smooth weave of this night,
and to this moon, plump and golden,
flying with its light.

Part Four

HOW IT LOOKS AT YOU

You gaze at the traceries
of the iris, its velvet flares,
and you feel it again, beauty
looking back at you, so intimate
and so removed.

Even as you try words, or a needle
on tapestry, you fear it
as you love it. The mountains
changing their faces from rose
to blackish-purple in minutes,

the dragon-fly passing
in its shimmering armor,
the curves of a loved face
with its hidden bones, or
one line on a canvas, how

it draws you into its tense
secret, then drops you off
into nothingness. Today this iris
in a field of dry grass,
and you are remembering

classmates coming during a long
illness with a gift,
a miniature tabernacle,
how they set it on the desert
of your sheets, and you sat up,

cheeks burning, lifted
the eleven layers of curtains
one by one, crimson, purple,
blue, and underneath, the tiny table
for bread, the candlestick,

the veil parting on a string,
and then, at last, the golden eye
with its holy, holy.

TO WILL ONE THING

for my brother Orlando Wiebe
                    (1919-1971)

My earliest memory of you:
watching you shave at the mirror,
that double image which you
defied to your last breath.
Singleness of heart, always diffused
by our needs, you would say.
And your bones told you so—
that April day the sharp pains
in your ribs, the diagnosis, and then
the months of grasping and opening.
The burial, the silence.

Oldest brother, bright one, quickest
of us all, I couldn't ease your
suffering. And that last night
your breathing rough and loud
as a beast's, the black tunnel
taking you in, and that knowledge
too deep for speech. One of your last
words to me—your face ash-yellow,
your lips dry—was "magnanimous,"
your description of one you loved.
I was standing by your bed, swollen
with life, my unborn child taking
from me everything it needed.
"To will one thing" became as large
as all of heaven and earth, or,
the mirror within the mirror
within the mirror, your face in it,
endless and diminishing.

RIVER

Beside the roar,
this stealthy, cushioned
walk. Over us, the silent
trees opening their leaves
so slowly, no one
witnesses it.
And that still pool
just beside
the swiftness
is that miniature life
you and I created as children
when twigs were trees
and folded paper a safe
boat for the stick man.
We turn our backs
to the river, but
when I look
at you I see it
side-glance
racing past your head.
We both know
about the falls
plunging not far below,
and above us, the white
beauty of the cascades.
We hear the music,
its great laughter
and its sobs. Symphonies.
Poulenc's "Gloria."

Even this placid
pool settles
into that risky flow,
and the roots,
the sucking roots
of those quiet trees,
keep reaching for it.

for Loren

EVEN UNDER THIS SUN

Today as the sun makes
its pure demands, its ruthless
searches, it seems that the earth
willingly gives itself up. The hills
lie down, tawny as lions, not a stir
from the grassy manes, while in the garden

yellow roses slowly open and curl,
brittle by noon, like parchment
that documents the day. The same sun
that Memorial Day, the year 1940,
when the parade glazed its way
to the cemetery, my organdy skirt

wilting as I watched in the swelter
of noon, and you waved to me as you
carried the tuba. I remember how
it nearly blinded me, light catching
and multiplying in the great bell,
Souza's hope blown into the biggest horn

you could find, ores pulled from the veins
of the earth, purified and shaped
so that the land could sing. You
nearly grown, pumping your breath into
a twist of brass that opened like
a giant lily, unwithered, growling

and belching under the piping
of the piccolo. Sounds that return to me
today, as though the hills, even under
this sun, desire to stir and to begin
again. As though something
still waits to be found.

for Arno

THIS EARTH

When the floor rolls
    and the lamps sway,
        I yell, "Earthquake!"
    and we all head out the door.
We gasp as the house
    finishes its shudder
        and for nights afterward
    lie fitfully on our floating beds.
In my grandfather's book,
    Last Times, everything quaked
        and swayed, whole families fell
    into a deep crevasse, screaming.
All humanity on a road,
    and the road split open.
        In 1902 grandfather preached
    Christ's imminent return.
Even then he headed north
    with his family. The train
        swayed with machinery, cattle, and bags
    of seeds toward the virgin prairie
which lay open and ready,
    enough for seven sons.
        This earth
    rolling, tipping, tumbling
us on, my grandfather now asleep
    in the hold, and I on deck,
        eyes straining, my whole self
    a pendulum, and the sun
every evening shuddering
    and dropping like a gong.

SINGING YOURSELF TO DEATH

From behind the library table
the cricket chants
his measured mating song,
and then you at the piano,
as if in answer.
Beethoven, I think,
with its insistence.
Not to be outdone,
the cricket shrills above
the pianissimo, holding forth
against the simultaneous
shimmering tones.
But at the grandest chords
his voice is drowned
and soon forgotten.
Finished with the journey
of themes and recapitulations,
you close the book
and there he is at your feet
on his back, legs flailing
in desperation or a last ecstasy,
dying with the old unsolved riddle
under this giant music maker
for whom he gave his best music,
for whom it would never
be good enough.

DRIVING IN FOG

The car has wings
in this low glide,
a soft layer of hiss
between me and the road.
A white wafting.
Intersections blurred,
the orchards swimming beside.
So this is the journey
above land, this easy thrust
into a tunnel of angelic
haze, tires barely grazing
the bosomy roll.
Skimming along the slow,
veiled fields, the fence-bound
stubborn roots. Gliding past
those heavy thighs which lean
against the doorjambs of heaven.

ONE FOR THE ROAD

Rooted to my skin
and to the crust
of this earth. How to travel
lightly with one foot
firmly tapped down?
Is this a one-legged dance,
this journey?

The ivy has a million
thirsty feet.

The young widow embraces
the bag of burned bones
and cries out.

My body thirsts for you.
Kiss me, pilgrim,
on the hills and in
the valley. I want
to gather armfuls
before I arrive.

TODAY

Adam's rib
is light.
Full of love,
I float
up to the ribs
of the cathedral
in easy, vertical line.
And the sun floats down,
colors the pale pillars,
ignites a saint's
carved curls,
even the wings
of gargoyles,
and the sword
over the stone-bent
couple at the gates.
And today
Chagall's fish
still flies,
dragging the clock.
His angel, heavy
with breasts,
stays aloft.
But the floating
lovers lie
at last
in Vava's lap.
Her face

is green with life,
and when she lifts
her rib cage to sing,
the inner plumb line
stretches
and the lead weight
swings.

for Jill

LAST SUMMER

He knows
it is his last
summer, sits
once more
in the late light
which trails down,
green as a willow.
His heart walks
unsteadily after
the wild dance
that crowded
his chest, pushing
against his throat.
In the embryo
the heart
is a dark dot
under the mouth,
close enough
to be swallowed.
Soon it branches out
like an oak,
upside-down,
leaves opening
in the skin.

And now, residues
of suns and moons
drift
in his thinned arteries,
and a distilled rain,
his heart high
and wavering.
A tree floating
in the pale light
of trees,
drinking
the air.

AFTER THE PRUNING

The vineyard has never
been so clean. Stripped
to the elemental, now air
and light enter full-shaft

where last autumn all
was weight and must
in the dusty shade. And where
the knife cut with its double

edge, all is delicacy and lift,
a jig in the breeze, as though
no terrors exist, as though
nothing could stop

the green flow now that
the dead and unnecessary
is gone, now that the wounded
eyes have healed shut.

Even night unlocks its iron
gates and allows the moon
to enter the vineyard where she
spreads her white gown
and loosens her hair.

JANUARY HAPPINESS

I burn the sweet burdens
of cedar, touch the rough

stiffness of the loquat
still green after frost.

Low sun rises over
the red barn where the horse

bumps after yesterday's
disciplines. Creekbed

is littered with tires
and bedsprings, a few muddy pools

for the fat muskrat
and a congregation of mallards

that refuses my crusts.
New buds on the Chinese tallow

the color of rust.
I walk over the bridge

of January, narrower
this year, walk over

the silent flow, my head
singing jazzy rhythms

above my dissolving feet.

Jean Janzen, daughter of Henry and Anna Schultz Wiebe, was born in Saskatchewan, Canada, in 1933. She lives in Fresno, California, with her husband, Louis, has four grown children and four grandchildren.

After completing her studies at Fresno Pacific College, Janzen graduated from California State University, Fresno with her Master of Arts. Previous publications include *Words for the Silence* (1984) and her poems in *Three Mennonite Poets* (1986).